"The Visit"

by Garry Somers

illustrated by Jamie B. Wolcott

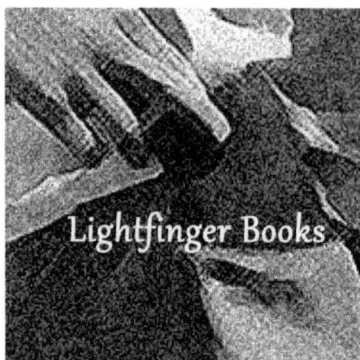

Lightfinger Books

Published by **The Blotter Magazine,** Inc.

Text copyright 2015 by Garrison Somers

Illustrations copyright 2015 by Jamie B. Wolcott

First Printing 2016

This is a work of fiction.

Any similarity or resemblance to persons living or dead is merely coincidental.

ISBN: 978-0-9839022-5-6

Published in the United States by Lightfinger Books, an imprint of The Blotter Magazine, Inc. 1010 Hale Street, Durham, NC 27705.

Printed and bound in the USA.

"The Visit"

Garry Somers
Illustrated by Jamie B. Wolcott

Dedicated to My Old Man.
GS

It were the wolf's night,
        when the dark stays its longest,
and I hacked extra kindling 'gin the cold.

Over the past days the wife had caulked the worst
      of the rain-leaks with mud-n-straw
                  so the damnable wind
     don't pluck the life from us
        while we sleep.

I bindled the three healthy ewes into the shed
and hobbled tother,
the ailin' ram with split horn,
to the foot of our bed
where it stopped blatting later a
short while.

T'weren't dead, tho' I
thot it might be.

My eldest lad propped his sack
          against the door to keep it to,
and the youngers tangled each other up
               in a straw-manger
while they mumbled wit sleep hunger
          after sharin' a bowl
               a sour pumpkin brot'.

Ma tucked her feet into her jacket

and I took my boots and staked them
near the firepit to dry,

and I finally shut my eyes
                when there was a fearful racket
        in the deadfall of gums
                        at forest's edge.

    The hell, I blasphemed
                        under me breath
    and groped 'round for the cudgel,
                the one with iron nail
                        stickin' point-out at the tip;
        it's no broadsword, mind,
            but will get a job done.

With no light
but the last bit of char from the soup
I peered out
'tro a chink in the sill,
couldn't see past the length of an arm
into the black.

The wind and snow burned at my eyes
and I hear'd summat crunch on the hoarfrost,
stompin' about wit' no fear,
like the very damned imp himself.

Then musts be a cloud slipped
        from betwixt the moon and me,
    I clapped my glance
        on a being not made for this world,

something carved by rain and rot
                    and left to wander
long after mortal breat' is lost.

It made me blood cold
and I spat sour from me mouth.

E'en by moonlight,
I could see he was enormous,
scary and wild hair'd.

Open yon door, the feller shouted,
  and I shook my head,
          as if he could see
        through the wall of me hut,

but I lost all taste for going out to thrash him,
          for I sensed
            that I could wail with my cudgel
and he'd let it snap across his beam,
          then tear me limb from limb.

Best open yon door, he growled again,
a sound like a bear makes
when it finds your stink
or that of your goat or sheep
on the breeze.

I couldn't have been no colder
had I stood out there myself and
still I know'd only a fool
would crack that door for somethin' in the night,

but I nudged my boy out of the way
                with my toe
                        and pulled it open.

        He ducked through the jamb
                as if cave stalking a rogue wolf,

    in one hand an ironwood branch,
                the tip hewed down to a point,
                        stained with mud
        and somethin' darker
        that ran just as foul
                into his scrofulous beard.

The other totin' a sack of some sort,
        seepin' gore.

From his belt hung a cleaver with antler handle.
He were tall enough to twist his neck
    so's not to bash his head on the rafters,
   and his eyes were as dark as a snake's.

A deep and dirty scar creased his brow,
    his nose and his cheek before
   hiding somewhere in his whiskers.

He spared nae e'en a look at me
                    but went right to work,
                            tromping to the firepit
            and kicking the ashes to red.

From the sack he tugged a man's severed leg.

You bloody butcher, I gasped in spite of meself.
What manner of foulness have you brought on this house?

But laying a stinking finger aside of his nose
he smiled and I felt the chill
through to my backbone.

No taste for venison? he grumbled.
I s'pose no when it's the burgomeister's deer.

Well, call me thief if ye mus,
but I dinna leave food on the hoof
what saunters past my sleepin' tree.

And he skewered the haunch on his branch
                    and propped it over the hot ashes
            where it sizzled and smoked
nd stank up the room something forgotten and lovely.

        Gor, I said, *I thot, that is, I thot I saw...,*
                    but in my hunger I lost the words
                for explaining what it was I'd been thinking.

Ne'er mind he mumbled and hunkered agin the wall.
            Wiped his scarred face.
                                Call me Nick.
I 'preciate yer lettin' me eat out from under the weather.

He pointed his thumb at the ailin' ram.

Are ye barm not atin yer sheep?

Nay I replied,
We take the wool in woolin' season for cash money,
though should the ill one die
we'll eat foine for couple week
and grind the bone into meal for spring garden.

But, I shrugged, *that'll be the end of the flock,*
with no new lambs.

Pity, he said under his breath.

Then me eldest woke up
          from the odor of roastin',
didn't even look at the strange feller
          for keepin' his eyes on the meat
    lest it disappear in this dream
                    he'd found himself in.

The little ones mewled like strays
while Ma peered sleepy around the bedcloth,

and I listened to Nick talk,
  though it were more like distant thunder
  than a man's voice:

Dark and difficult times we share,
  where pain is a common coinage,
  most of us hungry and lorn,
  the rest as evil as we are allowed
and if'n we only choose to see what's ours
  we all slip towards perdition
  wit' nothing to stem the fall.

And he smiled crookedly,

and what a twinkling earlier
        had sent a chill to me bones
now kicked a cold ash to life in my belly.

I got somethin' here I think you'll take a shine to,
        and he reached into his coat
and took out a small pouch.
It were tied with a thong and he worried it open
        with thumb and forefinger
and plucked a bit of summat into his palm.

'Twere a stone of a sort;
        he mashed it into powder
and sprinkled it onto the roasting haunch.

     Salt? I asked half to meself.
     Salt, he rumbled.

I hadn't had such in more'n a year,
        and the little ones, never.
   And Ma sometimes ate clay
        from a spot she knew near forest's edge
          just for a bit o' the savor.

Then he pulled his cleaver
    and sliced a portion as big as me hand.

    Tossed it to me.
I was so wobbly with hunger
        that I nearly fumbled it.
Couldn't wait but gnashed down.

      Gor, it was more than
        my jaws could take.

I smiled thanks and dribbled onto me shirt
it was so bloody good.

Then one for me eldest
who snatched it like a hound might,
another to me to hand back to the wife.

We ate in silence, then he carved again.

Two more pieces for the wee ones, he said.
Let 'em sleep, tho.

And he stood, his knees cracklin' as he stretched.
Pulled the meat from the branch,
shovin' it down in the old sack.
Wiped his greasy hand in his beard.

Best be off, he said. *Thanks for this.*

No, *stay,* I said, surprising meself again.
Too cold to be wanderin' about.

Nah, I'm used to it, he said
and clapped my shoulder with his paw
and it felt like a bear had swiped me a good one.

One more thing, he said,
and he tugged from his pocket a handful of black rocks
and flung them in the fire,
where they sparked to life.

You watch, he whispered, *they'll burn hot as the summer sun,
and longer than oak.*

And he pulled the door open,
        stepped through
                and yanked it behind him
ɔ's not that much wind was let loose in the room.

And I watched the fire grow
        and them rocks turnin' yellow
and dwelled on the wondrous peculiarment
        of being full and warm. ❖

Jamie B. Wolcott of Durham, NC, is a poster artist and illustrator. Her work resides in the place where these disciplines intersect. Using a rare watercolor technique that mimics glazing in oil paint, she creates vibrant and highly illustrative poster art for punk rock bands, revolutionary cabaret performers, vaudevillian lunatics and 20th century country music legends.

Garrison Somers is editor of The Blotter Magazine in Durham, NC. Lightfinger Books (an imprint of The Blotter Magazine, Inc.) are intended for use by folks sitting in waiting rooms where readers usually would prefer not to be where they are. Often, there isn't much to do to pass the time and take their minds off of those things that concern them most. We hope that these books help even a little bit with that very thing. If you would like to make a small donation to help offset production costs of this and other Lightfinger Books, check us out on www.blotterrag.com.

We hope you enjoyed reading yet another
micro-novel brought to you by
Lightfinger Books.

Collect 'em all & share with your friends.

For more information, to see our other
shenanigans, or to make a donation to our
cause, visit us at
www.blotterrag.com

Lightfinger Books

www.ingramcontent.com/pod-product-compliance
Lightning Source LLC
Chambersburg PA
CBHW060548030426
42337CB00021B/4485